PORT MOODY PUBLIC LIBRARY

D0603249

# simple stunning wedding
# SHOWERS

Festive Ideas and Inspiration for Perfect Pre-Wedding Parties

## Karen Bussen

Photographs by **William Geddes**

STEWART, TABORI & CHANG • NEW YORK

Editor: Jennifer Levesque
Designer: Susi Oberhelman
Production Manager: Jane Searle

Library of Congress Cataloging-in-Publication Data

Bussen, Karen.
    Simple stunning wedding showers / by
Karen Bussen ; photographs by
William Geddes.
        p. cm.
    Includes bibliographical references and
index.
    ISBN-13: 978-1-58479-540-7
    ISBN-10: 1-58479-540-9
    1.  Showers (Parties) 2.  Weddings.
3.  Simplicity.  I. Geddes, William, 1965-
II. Title.

GV1472.7.S5B87 2006
793.2—dc22        2006009489

Copyright © 2006 by Karen Bussen

All photographs are by William Geddes,
except the following:
Page 104 © Stephen Lovekin

Published in 2006 by
Stewart, Tabori & Chang
An imprint of Harry N. Abrams, Inc.

All rights reserved. No portion of this book
may be reproduced, stored in a retrieval
system, or transmitted in any form or by any
means, mechanical, electronic, photocopying,
recording, or otherwise, without written
permission from the publisher.

The text of this book was composed in
Helvetica Neue and New Caledonia

Printed and bound in China

10  9  8  7  6  5  4  3  2  1

HNA
harry n. abrams, inc.
a subsidiary of La Martinière Groupe

115 West 18th Street | New York, NY 10011
www.hnabooks.com

# contents

# INTRODUCTION
## Hosting a Simple Stunning Wedding Shower

The smaller celebrations that surround a wedding are all magical, special gatherings, but a bridal or wedding shower is one of the sweetest and most intimate of all the satellite celebrations. A shower is generally less formal than an engagement party, and it is often scheduled close to the big day, when excitement is building.

A wedding shower offers friends and family the chance to celebrate the bride, or the couple, at home or in a favorite setting, in a very personal way. The day is all about showering them with love, laughter, memories, and tokens of affection.

In my work as a party designer and planner in New York City, I've found that while a wedding generally involves numerous professionals—musicians, caterers, and the like—a wedding shower is almost always produced by a single friend or group of friends, in a very handcrafted, personal way. That's the beauty of this special event, but it can also be daunting for the host. Picking the right theme, organizing a guest list and invitations, creating a menu, and decorating with fitting details all require planning and imagination.

When it comes to creating your simple stunning shower, anything goes! The possibilities are endless and delightful. You could choose a dainty tea, a homey brunch, or a swanky cocktail fête. I've designed this book to help you, the host, create a party that is perfect for your guests and your honoree(s).

I'll guide you through each step, from setting a budget and determining proper etiquette to choosing the party style and selecting refreshments that will complement the ambiance. Along the way, I'll share ideas for inspired activities and stylish details to make your shower fun and unique.

This book follows the principles of my earlier book, *Simple Stunning Weddings*, in which I recommend choosing a focus or theme for your celebration, setting limits on colors and design elements, and layering with details that bring the look together.

I hope you'll find the food and drink recommendations helpful, and that you'll use the recipes not just for the wedding shower, but for any brunch, cocktail mixer, or dinner you host.

Throughout the book, the beautiful photographs by William Geddes each suggest a simple stunning idea for your party. To find the items in the photos, refer to the Resource Guide (page 107), which provides the names of vendors and Web sites that offer great party favors, games, decorations, and other accents.

So, let's start planning this fantastic party. Dream big, and let me help you with the details.

# getting STARTED

In the old days, a young woman would spend her youthful years collecting linens, china, and other objects to help her create a new home after marriage. Her family would also offer a sum of money, or a dowry, to the groom to offset the expense of setting up a new household.

But in old Europe, as the story goes, there was one pair of star-crossed lovers who weren't so lucky. Simply put, the bride's father, wealthy as he was, just didn't like the groom, who was a miller of very modest means. When the father refused to offer a dowry, the local townspeople, taking pity on the desperate couple, pooled resources to "shower" the bride with a sort of substitute dowry to make the couple's life together possible. And they lived happily ever after!

Did dad ever have a change of heart? Apparently he was so overwhelmed by the kindness of the strangers that he jumped on the bandwagon himself and wished the young lovers all the best. It seems safe to say the first bridal shower was a smashing success!

Today's version of the wedding shower is less of a make-it-or-break-it event, and more of an opportunity to shower the guest(s) of honor with love, good wishes, and gifts. Wedding showers nowadays aren't necessarily just for the bride. More and more, they are becoming coed events, where the bride and groom together are honored by friends and family. This also allows couples who are a bit older or who have already started their new homes to take part in the celebration and mark this special moment on the way to their big day.

## who hosts a wedding shower?

Generally, a shower is hosted by a close friend of the bride, or by one or more members of the bridal party. Tradition dictates that family members of the bride avoid hosting, as their entertaining might send a message that the family is soliciting gifts. However, this rule is not always strictly followed, since sometimes a family member (with a large home, for example) might be better equipped to host the party than a bridesmaid or friend. It is also acceptable for the bridesmaids, for

Make your bride an everlasting "initial" wreath out of silk rose petals. Cut out your letter from a block of foam and use hot glue to attach the petals. Hang it on your front door as a warm welcome, and let your guest of honor take it home as a souvenir.

instance, to act as the official hosts—sending invitations, organizing activities, and so on—while the bride's sister, for example, throws the party itself.

Truth be told, these days just about anyone can host a wedding shower. A close coworker, a family friend, even a couple near and dear to the bride and groom—anyone with a flair for entertaining guests and a desire to celebrate this happy occasion can make a wonderful host!

## who's invited to a wedding shower?

Traditionally, close friends and family of the bride made up the guest list. Her bridesmaids, her mother, her sisters, aunts, and grandmothers, along with any other loved ones and special friends. The groom's mother is customarily also invited. Showers can be intimate gatherings of just a few close-knit guests, or they can include coworkers and members of the extended family. If you're not sure who to invite, consult the bride's mother or another relative or friend.

Nowadays, of course, the guest list for a wedding shower might include men. If you are hosting a coed affair, it's appropriate to invite the groom's attendants, his father and siblings, and any other dear friends or associates.

The only rule of etiquette which must be followed when it comes to invitations is this: Do not invite

Welcome to Helen's Shower!

guests to the shower unless they will be invited to the wedding. It's considered bad form to invite guests to any wedding-related celebration without including them in the big day. An exception can be made if the shower is given by an office associate, since the bride or couple may choose, for a variety of reasons, not to invite every coworker to the wedding itself.

Shower guests enjoy colorful drinks like the Rosé Wine Spritzer (left) and the Orange Blossom pictured above. For recipes, see the Mix It Up chapter, page 91.

# what happens at a shower?

A wedding shower usually includes three main elements:

1. **Refreshments.** A shower can take place in a restaurant, a home, a tea shop, or another spot the guest or guests of honor enjoy. But regardless of the location, refreshments must be provided. Food and drinks may be served from a buffet, passed on trays by waiters, or offered family style at table. A more formal shower might feature a sit-down luncheon, tea, or dinner.

2. **Fun activities.** Ice breakers help guests get to know one another. Quizzes can reveal who knows most about the bride or couple. Bridal bingo, ballroom dance lessons, and other diversions can enhance the party's fun and energy. The activities you choose should be compatible with your setting and your bride or couple's tastes. See the Inspired Fun chapter, page 101, for ideas.

3. **Gifts.** To "shower" the bride or couple, guests generally bring gifts which are opened during the party. These gifts might reflect the theme of the event, and they do not have to be expensive or fancy. Often the gifts are passed around from guest to guest so as to be admired and appreciated by all.

# the scoop on some sticky
## SHOWER SITUATIONS

Q. **The bride has a number of close friends and family with small children, but we want to keep the shower "adults only." How do we let parents know they should leave the kids at home?**

A. Address the invitation envelope only to the intended invitee(s). Tradition dictates that only those whose names appear on the envelope are invited. Do not have "adults only" printed on your invitation, but do feel free to explain your wishes if parents inquire.

Q. **Is the host of the shower required to give a gift to the bride or couple?**

A. Yes. A thoughtful homemade gift or something from the couple's registry would be a perfect choice.

Q. **Should gifts be mentioned in the invitation?**

A. Since one of the main purposes of a wedding shower is to bestow presents on the bride or couple, it is entirely appropriate to mention a theme or focus. For example, if you host a 24-Hour shower, you might specify a unique time of day or night in each invitation ("10:00 A.M." or "midnight") to help inspire guests in their gift decisions. If your celebration is a Bed, Bath, and Brunch Bash, your invitation can convey this theme politely. You should *not*, however, list any registry details in the invitation, and you should never ask for specific gifts. This information should be shared strictly by word of mouth when a guest inquires.

tip+

Make sure you know the couple's registry particulars, color preferences, and any other details that might be helpful to guests who want to buy the perfect gift. When you're asked for more information, feel free to be specific about sizes, details, and anything else you know.

# planning your BUDGET

## be creative, spend wisely

Hosting any kind of party can be costly. As the host of a wedding shower, you must provide a place to celebrate and all the accoutrements that will make your guests comfortable and happy—food and drinks, place settings, decorations, and activities, among other things.

Budgets can vary widely from shower to shower, but, traditionally, showers are relaxed and not-too-fancy affairs, so keep that in mind.

Consider your budget when choosing a location for your party. It may be less expensive to host a small shower at home, but you'll have to buy all the other items you need (and clean up everything at the end!). Holding the shower in a restaurant or café might be a great alternative if you can negotiate an all-inclusive price.

Whatever your party theme and location, you'll want to plan a budget to help keep you on track. This chapter is filled with tips, tricks, and expert advice to get you started.

# creating your simple stunning shower budget

1. **Gather information.** Speak with the bride, or her mom or sister, to find out how many guests you should expect. Determine whether the bride or couple has a particular shower theme or setting in mind. This knowledge will help you budget for details later.

2. **Establish who will pay for the shower.** Will you host the party on your own or in conjunction with a few friends or bridesmaids? Come up with a total budget that works for you. Once you've determined how much you want to spend, you can allot specific amounts to specific categories (decorations, food, etc.).

3. **Make a list of the areas that will require spending.** Elements to consider include: the venue, food, beverages, invitations, serving pieces (plates, glasses, etc.), activities, decorations, and music. Plan to allocate about half your budget to refreshments and the other half to the remaining categories.

With a growing number of Web sites dedicated to affordable party supplies, personalized guest favors like these monogrammed chocolate bars are just a click away.

4. **Keep track of expenses throughout your planning.** It's a good idea to buy a little notebook or to keep a document on your computer to help you track your costs. Hold on to receipts and mark them clearly, especially if you'll share expenses with a group. Check your running tally from time to time to make sure you're keeping your costs in line.

# five great money-saving ideas

1. **Use your resources.** If you have a super-creative friend in your group, invite her to create photo collages or simple flower arrangements for the party. If there's a budding chef among you (or a professional one!), ask if she'll prepare a special cake or snack to wow the crowd.

2. **Shop on the Internet.** There are so many great wedding Web sites where you can order personalized napkins, gift tags, and coasters at discount prices. You can also find boxes, bags, and lots of wonderful games and activities online.

3. **Don't feel obligated to print fancy invitations.** Stationery stores offer wonderful invitations you can put through your home printer, or you can make your own with a nice pen, a rubber stamp, fun labels, and

Please join us
for a
Flower Workshop Shower
in honor of

## Sophie Jones

March 11
12:30pm
New Eastbury Golf and Country Club

Given with Love by
Debra, Joy and Linda

Rsvp by February 18th
(440) 321-6106

some pretty paper. When designing your invites, keep your shower theme in mind and focus on three or fewer colors for best results.

4. **Dress up take-out foods.** Create a pan-Asian buffet of delights from your favorite Thai, Chinese, and sushi spots. Arrange them beautifully and make a homemade dipping sauce for dumplings or satays. This idea also works well for a dessert-themed shower with baked goods (cakes, cookies, and cupcakes) from your local grocery store and bakery.

5. **Transform things you have around the house.** Turn old glass vases into hurricane candle holders. Use mirrors as serving trays or table runners. Adorn invitations or decorations with paper or ribbon remnants from your gift-wrap drawer. Your home can be a great source when you're seeking creative ways to spruce up a party without spending a fortune!

tip

If you want to hold the shower in a restaurant, consider a luncheon or an afternoon cocktail party between lunch and dinner. Most good restaurants welcome the opportunity to serve a group during off-hours, and they often charge less or offer extras as an incentive.

Use your resources. If you have a friend with a green thumb, enlist her to help with a flower or gardening workshop shower. During the party, guests learn a new skill and get to take home the fruits (or blossoms) of their labor.

# stunningly SIMPLE

Planning a happy occasion such as a wedding shower should be fun and easy for everyone involved. Just remember that the secret recipe for creating a special party in a streamlined process involves two ingredients: inspiration and organization. No matter what kind of shower you design for your bride or couple, you'll want to allow plenty of time to envision your party mood, and then to plan, coordinate, and create all the details that will make it perfect.

Whether it's a ladies-only luncheon or a coed cocktail party you're designing, the ten tips and tricks in this chapter will help you keep your décor and theme focused. Let them guide you throughout the process of taking your simple stunning shower from dream to reality.

1. **Remember, it's all about the bride.** Start by thinking about the bride you're honoring, and create a party that suits her personality. If you're hosting a coed shower for the couple, design the celebration to reflect their love and their style.

2. **Use your chosen theme throughout.** Once you've selected a theme for your party, incorporate it in your invitations, your color choices, and the foods and drinks you serve. If your bride isn't really a "theme" person, just make the bride or the couple your theme. Copy fun photos of her from over the years, use their first initials on a welcome wreath, and make her favorite dessert for the buffet.

3. **Don't overdo it: Limits are good.** Less is nearly always more. For a perfectly polished look, stick to no more than three colors in your party space. Also limit the number of materials and decorative elements to three in order to achieve a strong visual impact. For example, if you hang lanterns or other decorations, use no more than three shapes or sizes, and cluster them together. If you arrange centerpieces, use a maximum of three varieties of flowers in each vase.

Use color as a tool: Drape fabric or inexpensive sheets in your theme colors over couches and chairs. Buy some fun throw pillows to match your design, and toss them here and there. Serve drinks in pink, or peach, or your chosen hue. And look for candles and vases that coordinate (try the sale aisles at local home stores). These little details will make your party pop!

4. **Be in the clear.** Take a close look at the space where you'll be hosting the shower, and make sure there's ample space to mingle. You want guests to be able to move easily between seating areas and the buffet and bar. Remove any valuable pieces that could get damaged, and add a few small tables where your guests can rest a drink or plate without worry.

5. **Pack a punch with focused décor.** Select a few key areas to decorate for the strongest visual effect. A buffet or dining table, for example, is a great focal point—make it fabulous! Entrances and coffee tables are also perfect spots to accent; adorn them with candles, wreaths, pretty flowers, or paper wedding bells.

6. **Be prepared.** It may sound obvious, but make sure you have enough glasses, plates, and napkins for

A pretty package goes a long way. Colorful gift bags with a flourish of festive tissue make even a simple guest favor extra special.

everyone, along with garbage bags, hand towels, and toilet tissue. For a cocktail party, allot at least three paper napkins per guest, and two wine or cocktail glasses. Consider backing up with rental or plastic glassware, just in case, or you might find yourself doing dishes during the festivities.

7. **Combine homemade with ready-made.** Do not attempt to create every single hors d'oeuvres and flower arrangement from scratch. Use pretty plants to decorate. Visit your grocer's gourmet section and choose cheeses, breadsticks, olives, fruits, salads, and side dishes to accent your menu. Unless you are an experienced cook, make just a few special things yourself—and focus on recipes you've made before.

8. **Plan fun activities.** Involve your guests—and the bride or couple—in the fun by coming up with creative games and activities. Check out the chapter titled Inspired Fun (page 101)—it's filled with ideas to help you amuse and delight everyone at the party.

9. **Get help.** If you're going to host a shower for more than just a few people at your home, you might want a few extra hands to help with preparing and setting up. The hours just before a party are stressful, and time seems to fly. Ask a couple of friends to come early to help set tables or arrange your buffet and flowers. Also, consider hiring a waiter or a couple of local college kids to help with serving and cleanup. Designate a

space to put dirty dishes or rubbish—organizing these details in advance will save you time and trouble during the party and afterward.

10. **Appoint someone to take photos throughout.** Ask a creative friend to capture all the fun memories on film: Take pictures of the room décor before the guests arrive; get great shots of the bride as she opens her gifts. Then you can make the bride or couple a keepsake album or scrapbook, and you can share your snapshots online with everyone who attended.

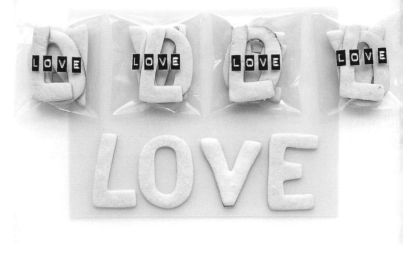

To save time and money, serve your favorite take-out foods in pretty bowls (opposite). Simple sugar cookies become sweet messages when you use letter-shaped cookie cutters to create home-baked guest favors (above).

# choosing a THEME

Traditionally, bridal showers were daytime, ladies-only luncheons or teas, which generally followed a similar format: refreshments accompanied by the opening of gifts. That classic concept still works beautifully for the right bride, but today the possibilities for designing a personal, unique party for a bride or a couple are only limited by your imagination.

The best way to begin planning a wedding shower (or a birthday or anniversary party, for that matter) is to think about the person or people you're celebrating. The bride or couple's personality, color preferences, and favorite foods can help inspire your party theme and all the details.

Your party's theme can take shape around a hobby or passion of the bride and groom, or it can center around their unique love story, whether they've known each other forever or met in an exotic locale. This chapter will help you organize your party checklist, and it will inspire you with twenty fabulous shower themes to consider for your celebration.

# shower planning checklist

Ideally you'd have at least two months to plan the wedding shower. If the party will take place very close to the date of the wedding, make sure to start planning even earlier, as the weeks leading up to the big day might be busy for you, and for those who will help you with cooking, decorating, and other details.

## TWO MONTHS BEFORE THE SHOWER:

☐ **Determine who will host the festivities.** Just you? Or will you have cohosts?

☐ **Set a budget.** Make a list of the folks who'll contribute and how much they'll chip in.

☐ **Choose a date.** Make sure to check the bride's or couple's schedule, too. If the shower is a surprise, ask someone close to them.

☐ **Create a guest list.** Consult with the bride or someone acquainted with her list of most treasured people, and make sure to check all addresses carefully.

☐ **Come up with a theme.** Use this chapter to help you and let your chosen theme inspire your menu, décor, and other party accents.

☐ **Prepare your invitations.** Allow extra time if you plan to have them printed professionally.

☐ **Hire professionals.** If you want musical entertainment or a fortune-teller or workshop instructor, book early.

## ONE MONTH BEFORE THE SHOWER:

☐ **Mail your invitations.** If you've created special invitations, make sure to check the postage requirements.

☐ **Design your menu.** Decide which dishes you'll make, and which you'll buy or order from a local restaurant. Place any orders for cakes and special wines, etc.

☐ **Plan your décor and details.** Order personalized items and guest favors, as well as any rental items you'll need, such as plates or glasses.

## TWO WEEKS BEFORE THE SHOWER:

☐ **Confirm orders for specialty items, such as cakes.** Also confirm the delivery or pickup arrangements.

☐ **Purchase any still-needed decorative items or supplies for activities.**

☐ **Divide last-minute tasks among cohosts.** Decide who will help put up decorations, prepare games, and so on.

## ONE WEEK BEFORE THE SHOWER:

☐ **Confirm your final guest count.**

☐ **Buy wines, liquors, and mixers.**

☐ **Buy groceries, and make a list of preparations.** Decide which items you can prepare in advance and start on those.

☐ **Confirm all deliveries one more time.**

☐ **Set the table and finish decorating the night before the shower, if possible.** This will save you headaches on the day of the party.

# 20 fresh shower THEME IDEAS

Following are twenty creative ideas for your simple stunning wedding shower. They're organized by time of day—starting with afternoon parties—and each includes a list of inspirations to help you pull it all together. Each shower features suggested menu items and drinks; you'll find the recipes in the chapters titled On the Menu and Mix It Up.

**HOW TO USE THIS SECTION:** Find the perfect theme and follow it through from start to finish, or feel free to mix and match foods, drinks, activities, and other elements from the different showers (and your imagination!) as they appeal to you. For example, your Comforts of Home party could easily be a brunch rather than a dinner, and you could serve your own favorite dishes and a few items from the Brunch Bests section of the On the Menu chapter. Some of the following themes, such as the Pampered Princess shower, are better suited for a ladies-only party, while others, such as the Cosmopolitan Mix cocktail hour shower, are designed for a coed celebration.

# bed, bath & brunch

### A CASUAL AFTERNOON OF FRENCH TOAST AND FINE LINENS

## INSPIRATION RELAXATION

**MOOD:** Relaxed, luxurious, practical, and pampered.

**SETTING:** At home or in a favorite restaurant or café.

**FOOD:** Anything you'd eat for breakfast (or brunch) in bed.

**RECIPES:** Aunt Maureen's Fluffy Egg Casserole, Quick Cranberry-corn Muffins, Nectar of the Goddess Yogurt Salad, Mini Peach Upside-down Cakes, Melted-chocolate Croissants, Princess Parfaits.

**DRINKS:** Bubbly Bride, Cava Cocktail, Rosé Wine Spritzer, Lillet Kiss, Orange Blossom, Hot Cha-cha-chocolate.

**ACTIVITIES:** Bed-and-bath Bridal Bingo (see page 102 for details on how to play). For more activities, see the Pampered Princess shower, page 41.

**DETAILS:** Order monogrammed hand towels for the guest bathroom or personalized cocktail napkins. Fill the bathtub in the guest bathroom with candles or flowers (or bottles of champagne!).

**GIFTS:** Monogrammed robes and slippers, pajamas, bed linens, breakfast trays, bubble bath, books (to read in the tub or in bed), and magazine subscriptions.

Wrap her in a soft, fluffy robe and serve her a bright blue Bubbly Bride cocktail. Then watch while she opens up gift boxes filled with monogrammed bed linens and luxurious towels. Serve your favorite homemade brunch treats or order fancy floral cupcakes from a local bakery. Offer guests scented hand soaps as favors.

*Tropical Rose*

# tea & table

This celebration is classic and elegant, but it doesn't have to be stuffy. Our version is an heirloom-inspired tea party, but you could easily translate the concept to feature Asian teas and sweets if it better suits your bride. Ladies love a tea party, with its light fare and pretty china. And just imagine the lucky guest of honor opening all sorts of wonderful treasures for her dining table!

## DAINTY INSPIRATION

**MOOD:** Vintage, sweet, romantic, classic, and elegant.

**SETTING:** At home or in a hotel or restaurant that offers tea service.

**FOOD:** Scones, finger sandwiches, canapés, and petits fours.

**RECIPES:** Tarragon Chicken Tea Sandwiches, Cucumber Canapés, Princess Parfaits, Mini Peach Upside-down Cakes, Green-tea Cake, Melted-chocolate Croissants.

**DRINKS:** Fine teas—hot and/or iced, Strawberry Green-tea Cooler, Rosé Wine Spritzer, Lillet Kiss, Orange Blossom, White-cranberry Spritzer.

**ACTIVITIES:** Set up a tea bar and let ladies create their own blends to drink or to take home as favors. Start a keepsake album during the shower: Take a photo of each guest, then ask her to write a favorite memory of the bride on a page marked with her name. After the party, print and arrange the photos to accompany each guest's note, and give this precious book to the bride to cherish.

**DETAILS:** Order monogrammed paper napkins or sugar cubes with the bride's initials. Pick up mix-and-match cups and saucers at flea markets to use for your tea service or to give as guest favors.

**GIFTS:** Linen napkins, napkin rings, place mats, dessert plates, cordial glasses, candy dishes, ice cream bowls, cake stands, and teapots.

# white magic

## INSPIRATION IN WHITE

**MOOD:** Light and airy, fresh and crisp, classic or modern.

**SETTING:** Daytime, at home or in a bright party space.

**FOOD:** Salads and sandwiches, or snacks and sweets.

**RECIPES:** Cucumber Canapés, Nectar of the Goddess Yogurt Salad, Nutty Goat-cheese Morsels, Smoked Salmon Roll-ups, Mini Peach Upside-down Cakes, Princess Parfaits.

**DRINKS:** White wine, vodka, clear sodas, sparkling water, Cava Cocktail, Saketini, White-cranberry Spritzer.

**ACTIVITIES:** Play Bridal Charades with clues about the guest of honor (see the chapter titled Inspired Fun for how to play), and give small white prizes, such as candy or soaps, to the winning team. Make a white album. Fill a handmade white book with black-and-white photos of guests, scraps of ribbon, souvenirs of the day, and happy wishes.

**DETAILS:** Drape couches with white sheets. Decorate with a few stems of white tulips or calla lilies. Light scented white candles to perfume the air.

**GIFTS:** Anything white: vases, plates, salt and pepper shakers, guest towels, accent pillows, picture frames, bathrobes, slippers, bath salts, scented candles.

Perhaps the most symbolically "bridal" of showers, this classic party is a celebration of all things crisp and bright and purely white. Against a beautiful backdrop of white linen on a buffet overflowing with pretty white cakes and sweets, the woman of the day opens gifts of crisp bed linens, downy pillows, serving platters, and silk pajamas, all in radiant, glorious, uplifting white. Of course, if you have a bride who's all about red (or green or blue, for that matter), the concept can translate beautifully.

*idea*

Encourage your guests to dress all in white. Suggest white hats, shoes, scarves, and accessories. At the party, take a vote and award a prize to the loveliest (or most creative) lady in white.

# hours of flowers

A WORKSHOP SHOWER IN FULL BLOSSOM

Workshop showers offer guests a chance to learn something new while sharing a fun, festive activity with friends and family.

For the Hours of Flowers variety, enlist a florally inclined friend, or better yet, a florist, to host a how-to on floral care and design. Guests make arrangements in simple vases, and then take them home as party favors. For the bride, gifts of garden goodies delight.

**idea**

A great workshop shower can center on any activity. Hire a ballroom dancer to show the girls how to cut a rug at the wedding. Schedule experts to demonstrate how to decorate perfect cookies or wrap beautiful gifts. Use your imagination, and design a workshop that's right for the guests on your list.
To save on fees, consider hiring advanced baking students or teaching assistants rather than their higher-paid bosses.

## BLOOMIN' GOOD INSPIRATION

**MOOD:** Fun, interesting, creative, artistic, and natural.

**SETTING:** At home or in a flower shop.

**FOOD:** Light lunch or brunch dishes, with edible flower accents.

**RECIPES:** Aunt Maureen's Fluffy Egg Casserole, Quick Cranberry-corn Muffins, Panini Hearts, Tarragon Chicken Tea Sandwiches, Mini Peach Upside-down Cakes.

**DRINKS:** Rosé Wine Spritzer, Cava Cocktail, Lillet Kiss, Bubbly Bride, White-cranberry Spritzer, Orange Blossom.

**ACTIVITIES:** Play Pin the Boutonniere on the Groom. Photocopy a picture of the groom onto a large piece of paper. Try to get your hands on a picture of him in a suit, or cut and paste his head on top of a magazine photo of a movie star in a tuxedo. Then make a "boutonniere" out of construction paper. Blindfold the bride and guests, spin them around, and give a prize to the person who gets the flower closest to his left lapel.

**DETAILS:** Add edible flowers to ice cubes and salads. Print out floral-tip sheets to help guests remember what they've learned. Ask the workshop leader to make a small bouquet for the bride to take home.

**GIFTS:** Garden tools, flower books, herbal hand lotions, floral-scented candles, seed packets, and vases.

# bubbly brunch

## EFFERVESCENT INSPIRATION

**MOOD:** Festive, convivial, casual yet elegant.

**SETTING:** At home or in a favorite restaurant.

**FOOD:** Pancakes and eggs, or crêpes and caviar.

**RECIPES:** Aunt Maureen's Fluffy Egg Casserole, Quick Cranberry-corn Muffins, Panini Hearts, Smoked Salmon Roll-ups, Tarragon Chicken Tea Sandwiches, Melted-chocolate Croissants.

**DRINKS:** Prosecco, cava, champagne, cider, or any other sparkling beverage you adore. Cava Cocktail, Prosecco Pomegranate Punch, Rosé Wine Spritzer, Orange Blossom, White-cranberry Spritzer.

**ACTIVITIES:** Offer up a Rhyming Toast Challenge. On your invitation, ask guests to prepare a short rhyming toast to the bride and groom, which they'll share at the party while raising a glass of bubbly. You can also give guests paper, pen, and five minutes to compose their toasts at the shower.

**DETAILS:** Use a bubble theme on your invitations. Give small bottles of bubble bath as guest favors. Fill glass vases with clear marbles and a few whimsical flowers.

**GIFTS:** Barware, home accessories, books about bubbly, champagne glasses, wine stoppers, and wine buckets.

You can host this festive shower as a formal champagne brunch or as a more casual tasting of some of the world's great, but lesser-known, sparklers paired with hors d'oeuvres and finger foods. Match your theme and menu to your couple's favorite bubbles. This shower works well with any gift theme, such as "bar," "home," or "bed and bath," and is perfect for a coed celebration.

idea

Set up a bubbly bar with sparkling wines, juices, and mixers, such as Lillet (an orange-infused aperitif) or Chambord (a raspberry liqueur). Add bowls of fresh blueberries and raspberries to drop in as a fun, fruity garnish.

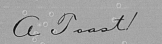

*A Toast!*

JOIN US FOR A BUBBLY BRUNCH

IN HONOR OF

*Nadia and Thomas*

SUNDAY, THE SEVENTH OF MAY

11:30AM

TWO HORATIO STREET

NEW YORK CITY

• • •

GINNY HARTMAN, MARIE VAZ, AND JAMES DYSON

KINDLY REPLY TO 212.561.8900

# organic botanic

## EARTHY INSPIRATION

**MOOD:** Handmade, one-of-a-kind, creative, and natural.

**SETTING:** At home or in a garden.

**FOOD:** Farmers' market finds and homemade classics.

**RECIPES:** In the chapter titled On the Menu, anything from Brunch Bests, Finger Foods, Buffet Favorites, or Sweet Treats.

**DRINKS:** Organic wines, fresh juices, herbal teas. Rosé Wine Spritzer, Cava Cocktail, Strawberry Green-tea Cooler, Orange Blossom, White-cranberry Spritzer.

**ACTIVITIES:** Make a Bridal Shower Scrapbook. See page 105 of the Inspired Fun chapter for easy instructions. Sponsor a "recycled wrapping" contest and give a prize to the guest with the greenest (most earth-friendly) gift wrap.

**DETAILS:** Decorate in shades of green or in natural hues. Use recycled pickle jars as vases or glasses. Print invitations on recycled paper and choose an "earth" or "garden" theme. Give organic-seed packets as guest favors or make a donation to the bride's favorite eco-cause.

**GIFTS:** Garden tools, cookbooks, books about composting or farming, dinnerware made from recycled wood or ceramic, and anything handmade.

More and more folks are taking an interest in all things organic and environmentally healthy. This party celebrates the bride or couple who delights in farmers' markets, composting, hybrid cars, and recycled products. Host it as a brunch, afternoon tea, or family-style dinner, and forego plastic forks and Styrofoam in favor of recycled party supplies.

tip

If you decide to cook for an organically inclined couple, use as many organic foods as you can find. Vegetables, fruits, cheeses, even spices— many great choices are available at specialty grocers (and some mainstream stores). Any of the recipes in this book can easily be made with organic ingredients.

# pampered princess

AN AFTERNOON OF BEAUTY AND BEST FRIENDS

Is your bride a princess? Or does she deserve to be treated like one for a day? Crown her with a festive tiara and treat her to hours of spa services and gifts. This shower can be more expensive for your guests if they join you for massages and manicures, but many spas do offer special group rates and packages for bridal showers. If you host this shower at home, ask guests to bring their robes and slippers so they'll be comfy and relaxed!

**idea** If you choose to celebrate a spa day at home, hire a professional or two to help make it special. A massage therapist might offer ten-minute chair massages or foot rubs, while a beauty specialist might give mini facials, eyebrow touch-ups, or makeup demos.

## ROYAL INSPIRATION

**MOOD:** Luxurious, feminine, healthy, and relaxing.

**SETTING:** At home or in a spa or salon.

**FOOD:** Spa fare: veggies and dip, salads, light sandwiches.

**RECIPES:** Nectar of the Goddess Yogurt Salad, Quick Cranberry-corn Muffins, Cucumber Canapés, Tarragon Chicken Tea Sandwiches, Smoked Salmon Roll-ups, Nutty Goat-cheese Morsels, Green-tea Cake, Princess Parfaits, Melted-chocolate Croissants.

**DRINKS:** Fizzy water with lemon, wine spritzers, sake, and fresh juices. Lillet Kiss, Cava Cocktail, Rosé Wine Spritzer, Orange Blossom, Hot Cha-cha-chocolate.

**ACTIVITIES:** Set up a Goddess Goodies Bar brimming with girlie guest favors. (See page 47 for inspiration.) Invite every guest to bring a "recipe" or idea for a home beauty treatment, and make a Beauty Secrets book for the bride.

**DETAILS:** Use flowers, soft music, and scented candles to create a relaxing mood.

**GIFTS:** Skin care products, bath beads, slippers, robes, pajamas, candles, spa gift certificates, subscriptions for magazines (to read in the bathtub!), and anything relaxing or beauty enhancing.

# love, sweet love

## MORSELS OF INSPIRATION

**MOOD:** Sexy, playful, luscious, and sophisticated.

**SETTING:** At home or at a fancy chocolate shop.

**FOOD:** White chocolate, dark chocolate, milk chocolate—the more, the better! Chocolate cakes, truffles, and cookies.

**RECIPES:** Decadent Chocolate Parfaits, Melted-chocolate Croissants, Lightning Chocolate Raspberry Cupcakes.

**DRINKS:** Bridal Sweet, Prosecco Pomegranate Punch, Mocha Liqueur Cups, Hot Cha-cha-chocolate.

**ACTIVITIES:** Play "She said what?" Appoint a guest to record the exact words the bride utters as she opens each present ("Oh my!" "Wow!" "I've never seen anything like it!"). When all the gifts are opened, read her phrases back out loud with the proper giggle-inducing emphasis—you want to sound like she might on her wedding night.

**DETAILS:** Decorate with sexy reds and pinks. Write your invitations in lipstick or include a chocolate kiss.

**GIFTS:** Slippers, shoes, stockings, sexy mood-enhancing CDs, nighties, undies, teddies, and jammies.

For the right bride, this shower is a perfect combination of sin and heaven. Somehow, chocolate and sexy underwear just seem to go together! The great thing about this bridal shower is that it can be crafted from homemade elements, such as the recipes suggested, or created entirely from store-bought confections—like these from world famous chocolatier Fauchon—to save time and trouble.

# double happiness

Asian-inspired parties can be super festive and colorful, or incredibly modern and serene. Choose what's best for your bride, and layer your party with inventive details to enhance your theme. Many Asian party decorations and favors, such as pretty slippers, are inexpensive, and can be found online (see the Resource Guide, page 107). If you're not much of a cook, you can create a sumptuous, reasonably priced buffet entirely from take-out foods. As for your gifts, think home, spa, or travel.

## ZENSPIRATION

**MOOD:** Casual, exotic, spicy, festive, or Zen.

**SETTING:** At home or in your favorite Asian restaurant.

**FOOD:** Dumplings, stir-fry, satay, pad thai, and sushi.

**RECIPES:** Lemongrass Shrimp Skewers, Smoked Salmon Roll-ups, Saffron Couscous, Green-tea Cake, Princess Parfaits.

**DRINKS:** Thai beer, sake, or bubble teas. Saketini, Fred & Gingertini, Strawberry Green-tea Cooler, Orange Blossom.

**ACTIVITIES:** Include an attractive blank card or piece of paper in your shower invitation. Ask guests to write down a quote, thought, or bit of wisdom about love and marriage. Instruct them to bring the cards with them to the shower, and assemble a Wedding Wit and Wisdom Book for the bride as a special gift from her guests.

**DETAILS:** Buy personalized fortune cookies on the Internet. Give inexpensive slippers or chopsticks as guest favors.

**GIFTS:** Spa treatments, dinners for two, travel accessories, good-luck charms, tea, beauty and skin care products, and anything else that your bride would adore.

# bohemian bride

## DIVINE INSPIRATION

**MOOD:** Sexy, off-beat, funky, hip, and ethereal.

**SETTING:** At home or in a spa or her favorite café.

**FOOD:** Dried fruits and nuts, tapas, hummus and pita, or decadent treats and sweets.

**RECIPES:** Saffron Couscous, Lemongrass Shrimp Skewers, Bacon-wrapped Dates, Nutty Goat-cheese Morsels, Nectar of the Goddess Yogurt Salad, Green-tea Cake, Princess Parfaits.

**DRINKS:** Cava Cocktail, Saketini, Lillet Kiss, Rosé Wine Spritzer, Strawberry Green-tea Cooler, Orange Blossom.

**ACTIVITIES:** Hire a fortune-teller or a *mehndi* artist to paint guests' hands. Set up a Goddess Goodies Bar of indulgent favors, such as nail polish, bath beads, potpourri, aromatherapy oils, lip gloss, and incense. Let the ladies scoop their favorites into gift bags as a sumptuous souvenir of the day.

**DETAILS:** Give your party an Eastern theme—toss Indian throw pillows on the floor, serve drinks in Moroccan tea glasses, and add jewel-toned accents with favors of bangles and beads.

**GIFTS:** Incense, scarves, jewelry, perfume, artwork, poetry, books, music, and bubble bath.

What better way to shower your one-of-a-kind bride than to treat her to an afternoon or evening of eclectic foods and gifts to pamper her? This is a globally inspired celebration, full of spice and color, the air perfumed with incense, the mood enhanced by the sounds of soft music and the romantic glow of candles.

## did you know?

Hand and foot painting, or *mehndi* artistry, originates from India and other parts of South Asia. The artist paints intricate designs on the hands and/or feet of the bride and other women who desire to be adorned, using a natural henna-based ink. After drying, the designs—flowers, hearts, vines, and other symbols—remain intact from several days to a week as a magical memory. See page 104 for a picture of classic *mehndi* artistry.

# promises, promises

AN I-OWE-YOU SHOWER FOR THE COUPLE WHO COULD USE A HAND

## CAN-DO INSPIRATION

**MOOD:**  Simple, heartfelt, creative, and one-of-a-kind.

**SETTING:**  At home or in a cozy restaurant.

**FOOD:**  Brunch, cocktail snacks, or cozy comfort foods.

**RECIPES:**  In the chapter titled On the Menu, anything from Brunch Bests, Finger Foods, Buffet Favorites, or Sweet Treats.

**DRINKS:**  Cava Cocktail, Prosecco Pomegranate Punch, Bridal Sweet, Lillet Kiss, Fred & Gingertini, Orange Blossom, and Strawberry Green-tea Cooler.

**ACTIVITIES:**  Set up a homemade photo booth. Hang some fabric as a backdrop, then place a digital or Polaroid camera and a photo album nearby. Guests can take snapshots of each other and create a whimsical photo album with thoughts and good wishes.

**DETAILS:**  Make Can-Do Certificates to enclose with your invitations. Guests can choose what to promise, and you can collect all the certificates in a beautiful book for the couple to keep.

**GIFTS:**  Certificates promising to paint a study, organize a garage, help with a move, wallpaper a kitchen, tile a bathroom, or pet-sit the family critters.

This classic helping-hand shower encourages guests not to buy gifts, but rather to help the new bride or couple with a project or plan, such as remodeling their home or planting their garden. It's a hands-on gift-giving experience, and an opportunity to build not just a room or pool deck, but also precious memories and friendships to last a lifetime.

idea

Are your bride and groom more interested in lending a helping hand than receiving one? If so, try a fresh twist on the promise shower gift theme. Pledge your time or make a donation in the couple's honor to support their favorite charity or community-related cause.

# home rooms

AROUND-THE-HOUSE FUN WITH GIFTS AND GAMES

This is a popular shower theme and a practical one if the couple will be starting a new home together. In the invitation, each guest is assigned a room in the home as a gift inspiration. This idea works well for a brunch, cocktail party, or dinner, and it's delightful for a coed celebration. Remember, don't list registry information or specific gifts on your invitation. Etiquette says you should share gift preferences only when asked.

**idea**

To decorate your home-themed shower, make a welcome-mat centerpiece for your buffet. Buy a flat of fresh wheat grass from your local garden center or farmers' market. Use inexpensive flowers, such as daisies or button mums, to spell out the couple's initials or a sweet message.

## ROOMFULS OF INSPIRATION

**MOOD:** Whimsical, festive, and familial.

**SETTING**: At home or in a casual, family-style restaurant.

**FOOD:** Brunch, hors d'oeuvres, or serve-yourself favorites.

**RECIPES:** In the chapter titled On the Menu, anything from Brunch Bests, Finger Foods, Buffet Favorites, or Sweet Treats.

**DRINKS:** Bridal Sweet, Prosecco Pomegranate Punch, Cava Cocktail, White-cranberry Spritzer.

**ACTIVITIES:** Play At Home with the Bride and Groom. Prior to the party, ask the bride and groom questions about themselves: "What is your favorite room in the house?" "Where would you live if you could live anywhere?" Then, during the festivities, ask guests the same questions about the couple, and have them write down their answers. Whoever ends up with the most right answers gets a prize.

**DETAILS:** Use a house motif on your invitations. Stationery stores with scrapbooking sections offer lots of great stickers and charms to accent home-themed invitations, decorations, and gift wrap.

**GIFTS:** Kitchen tools, blankets for the bedroom, magazine racks, barware, laundry baskets, and car kits for the garage.

# that's entertainment!

## PLUGGED-IN-SPIRATION

**MOOD:** Casual and festive, vintage, or cutting-edge.

**SETTING:** At home or off-hours in a small local movie theater.

**FOOD:** Licorice, popcorn, and other movie-house staples.

**RECIPES:** Spicy Roasted Cocktail Nuts, Salty-sweet Cheese Popcorn, World's Best Mac-n-cheese, Decadent Chocolate Parfaits, Lightning Chocolate Raspberry Cupcakes.

**DRINKS:** Bridal Sweet, Fred & Gingertini, Prosecco Pomegranate Punch, Cava Cocktail, White-cranberry Spritzer.

**ACTIVITIES:** Play Wedding Singer Karaoke. Take turns belting out first-dance classics ("Open Arms," "At Last," "You're the First, the Last, My Everything") and give prizes for best ballad, rock, and disco classics. Or play Bride and Groom Favorites: quiz guests on the couple's favorite movies, music, and TV shows.

**DETAILS:** Write your invitations on old movie postcards with photos of classic couples from the stage and screen: Tracy and Hepburn, Bogey and Bacall, Fred and Ginger. Play movies or mixed CDs of the couple's favorite music in the background.

**GIFTS:** DVDs, CDs, video games, computer software, movie rental subscriptions, remote controls, shower radios, beanbag chairs, pajamas, and MP3 players.

Are your bride and groom classic movie buffs or sports fans? Do they watch their favorite TV shows religiously? Why not shower them with all the things they need to create a wonderful home theater and entertainment lounge?

**tip**

This entertainment shower can be put together with very little time and trouble. Order decorations and candies off the Internet (see the Resource Guide for more info). Throw some popcorn in the microwave, and stop by your local movie theater to pick up cute serving bags (or order custom bags with the couple's names from a party supply Web site). If you want to offer a full meal, make up a batch of the World's Best Mac-n-cheese in advance (recipe on page 78) and reheat it just before the party.

# on the town

## RECREATION INSPIRATION

**MOOD:** Unexpected, posh, hip, and unique.

**SETTING:** At home or in a lounge, bar, restaurant, or loft.

**FOOD:** Swanky snacks. Olives, cheeses, tapas, or sushi.

**RECIPES:** Smoked Salmon Roll-ups, Spicy Roasted Cocktail Nuts, Salty-sweet Cheese Popcorn, Beef Canapés with Horseradish, Nutty Goat-cheese Morsels, Bacon-wrapped Dates, World's Best Mac-n-cheese.

**DRINKS:** Prosecco Pomegranate Punch, Cava Cocktail, Rosé Wine Spritzer, Bridal Sweet, Fred & Gingertini, White-cranberry Spritzer.

**ACTIVITIES:** Create a Bride and Groom Scavenger Hunt around the house or neighborhood. Pick teams and have guests retrieve items that are special to the bride and groom (candy, a menu from their favorite local restaurant, and so on). The winning team gets movie passes or another small treat.

**DETAILS:** Make a dessert buffet inspired by the twosome's favorite movies. Hire a celebrity impersonator or magician to entertain guests.

**GIFTS:** Theater, sports, or concert tickets, museum memberships, dinner vouchers for two, amusement park passes, and spa gift certificates.

Is your couple the type that enjoys experiences more than objects? Throw them a leisure-time cocktail shower and give them passes for great things to do together—theater tickets, museum memberships, massage coupons, and more!

**idea**

For the couple who are constantly on the move, consider hosting a "progressive" party. Start with an appetizer hour and gift opening at your place, then move the party to a different spot (the couple's favorite restaurant, for example) for dinner and dessert. If you like the Bride and Groom Scavenger Hunt idea, have guests gather the items on their way to the second location.

# passport to love

This shower can be honeymoon related (gifts for their big trip) or more generally travel oriented—whichever you like. Choose a city, region, or continent that appeals to your couple, and layer your party with details reminiscent of their favorite spots.

## DESTINATION INSPIRATION

**MOOD:** Exotic, adventurous, sophisticated, and chic.

**SETTING:** At home or in a restaurant.

**FOOD:** Choose one exotic cuisine or create a global buffet.

**RECIPES:** Lemongrass Shrimp Skewers, Bacon-wrapped Dates, Beef Canapés with Horseradish, Tomato Bruschetta, Panini Hearts, Saffron Couscous, Green-tea Cake, Decadent Chocolate Parfaits.

**DRINKS:** Saketini, Cava Cocktail, Fred & Gingertini, Bridal Sweet, Lillet Kiss, Prosecco Pomegranate Punch, Orange Blossom.

**ACTIVITIES:** Travel True or False. This game reveals who knows most about the couple's travels. Before the party, ask the bride and groom questions about places they've visited. What was their favorite vacation ever? Have they been to Europe? For the party, create a list of true-or-false questions and give a prize to the guest with the most correct answers.

**DETAILS:** Design your invitations with the feel of a ticket or passport. Copy photos of the couple on favorite trips and display them on a welcome table or buffet.

**GIFTS:** Luggage, passport holders, travel wallets, sunglasses, maps, and guidebooks to exotic destinations.

Maps make great decorative accents for a travel-related shower. Wrap gifts or guest favors with colorful maps. Use them to line hors d'oeuvres trays or as table runners or place mats. Cover old glass or plastic vases with black-and-white maps. Then brush them with cold tea for a vintage look. Add a few flowers for a centerpiece, or use them to hold silverware on your buffet.

# cosmopolitan mix

This hip get-together is perfect for the couple who loves to entertain and be entertained. If your bride and groom are true foodies, consider hiring a top caterer. Manhattan-based Creative Edge Parties created this stunning shower in their Greenwich Village catering loft.

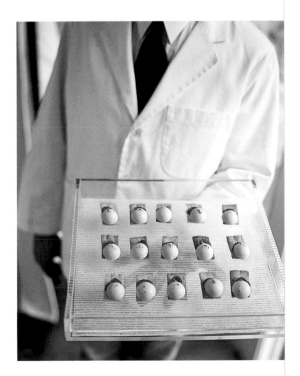

## INSPIRATION COCKTAIL

**MOOD:** Sexy, swanky, classic, or trendy.

**SETTING:** At home, in a beautiful bar, a loft, or a hotel lounge.

**FOOD:** Snacks and finger foods to suit your chosen setting.

**RECIPES:** Spicy Roasted Cocktail Nuts, Salty-sweet Cheese Popcorn, Smoked Salmon Roll-ups, Nutty Goat-cheese Morsels, Lemongrass Shrimp Skewers, Tomato Bruschetta, Bacon-wrapped Dates, Decadent Chocolate Parfaits.

**DRINKS:** Gimlets, Manhattans, and cosmopolitans. Fred & Gingertini, Saketini, Cava Cocktail, Bridal Sweet, Lillet Kiss, Rosé Wine Spritzer, Mocha Liqueur Cups, Orange Blossom.

**ACTIVITIES:** Rhyming Toast Challenge. See the Bubbly Brunch shower, page 38, for how to play.

**DETAILS**: Personalize cocktail napkins with variations on classic quotes: "Here's looking at you, kids!" or with timeless pairs (Antony and Cleopatra, Samson and Delilah, Romeo and Juliet). Set up a special theme bar with drinks tailored to your couple. Serve chic mini ice cream cones or other bite-sized desserts at the party's end.

**GIFTS:** Barware, glassware, cocktail recipe books, gadgets, and bottles of the couple's favorite libations.

# grape expectations

## INSPIRATION LIBATION

Raise a glass to the bride and groom with this shower designed to help them stock their wine cellar. You can host this party as a wine-and-cheese tasting, or as a sit-down feast with food-and-wine pairings. Many local wineries hold parties in private rooms, so check your local resources for options.

**MOOD:** Swanky, tasteful, elegant, and lush.

**SETTING:** At home or in a winery, wine school, or fine restaurant.

**FOOD:** Cheeses, meats, and exotic or indulgent ingredients.

**RECIPES:** Nutty Goat-cheese Morsels, Tomato Bruschetta, Smoked Salmon Roll-ups, Spicy Roasted Cocktail Nuts, Bacon-wrapped Dates, Beef Canapés with Horseradish, World's Best Mac-n-cheese, Sage-roasted Cornish Game Hens.

**DRINKS:** The couple's favorite varieties and vintages. Cava Cocktail, Rosé Wine Spritzer, Lillet Kiss, Prosecco Pomegranate Punch, White-cranberry Spritzer.

**ACTIVITIES:** Blind Tasting for the bride and groom. Cover a bottle of wine with a velvet wine bag so the label is hidden. Write down some notes about the wine (check the label or ask your wine merchant). Pour a taste of each for the bride and groom and ask them to identify the wine and/or its characteristics. The winner (whoever gives the best description) receives a bottle of champagne to share at home with the runner-up!

**DETAILS:** Use empty wine buckets or bottles as vases. Fill bowls with red and green grapes to create a simple centerpiece.

**GIFTS:** Wine openers and stoppers, books about wine, hand-blown wine glasses, subscriptions to wine magazines, and coasters.

tip

At the party, serve at least one wine your oenophile duo hasn't yet discovered. Brachetto d'Acqui, for example, is a delicious sparkling red dessert wine from Italy. It's slightly sweet and festively fizzy, and it tastes great with cake and chocolate. It's also reasonably priced! Check your wine store or the Internet for a good producer.

# 24-hour shower

GIFTS FOR A DAY-IN-THE-LIFE OF YOUR BRIDE AND GROOM

No, the party itself doesn't have to last that long! This shower is a variation on the Home Rooms concept, with time as its focus. Whether a ladies-only or coed fête, the object is to shower the guest(s) of honor with gifts to delight them from breakfast to bedtime.

## idea

Give your bride and groom a Time Capsule. Fill a beautiful box with items that will call to mind the year of their marriage—a CD of their current favorite band or a list of the top songs on the charts, a DVD of their best-loved movie of the year, shower souvenirs, photos of the group, and other small, personal items. They'll smile every time they open this treasure chest in the years to come.

## 24/7 INSPIRATION

**MOOD:** Casual or elegant, playful, creative, and practical.

**SETTING:** At home or in a club or private dining room.

**FOOD:** Choose your menu to suit the hour of your party, or mix snacks from different times of the day.

**RECIPES:** In the chapter titled On the Menu, anything from Brunch Bests, Finger Foods, Buffet Favorites, or Sweet Treats.

**DRINKS:** Bridal Sweet, Cava Cocktail, Fred & Gingertini, Rosé Wine Spritzer, Mocha Liqueur Cups, Hot Cha-cha-chocolate.

**ACTIVITIES:** Time Trivia—Ask the bride and groom in advance to answer some time-related questions about themselves. Then quiz guests on what time the bride gets up, what time of day the couple met, or how much time passed before he proposed. Play individually or in teams, and give prizes to the winners.

**DETAILS:** Put a clock face on your invitation, and assign each guest an hour of the day. The time noted (midnight or 8:00 A.M., for example) will serve as a gift inspiration.

**GIFTS:** Clocks, pajamas, lingerie, skin care or bath products, coffee mugs, midnight snacks, music or movies, and board games.

# gourmet soiree

## TASTY INSPIRATION

**MOOD:** Sumptuous, sophisticated, and delicious.

**SETTING:** In a fantastic open kitchen or dining room.

**FOOD:** Fancy cheeses, olives, breads, pâtés, or gourmet potluck favorites.

**RECIPES:** Spicy Roasted Cocktail Nuts, Smoked Salmon Roll-ups, Nutty Goat-cheese Morsels, Bacon-wrapped Dates, Beef Canapés with Horseradish, World's Best Mac-n-cheese, Sage-roasted Cornish Game Hens, Garlic-kick Mashed Sweet Potatoes, Gruyère-stuffed Dinner Rolls, Decadent Chocolate Parfaits, Mini Peach Upside-down Cakes.

**DRINKS:** Wine, microbrewed beers, sparkling cider, and cocktails. Cava Cocktail, Rosé Wine Spritzer, Fred & Gingertini, Lillet Kiss, Bridal Sweet.

**ACTIVITIES:** Test the bride and groom on their food knowledge. Create a multiple-choice quiz with questions like "What's the difference between a sauce and a gravy?" See the Comforts of Home shower, page 61, for more activities.

**DETAILS:** Use cutting boards as platters and mixing bowls or utensil caddies as vases.

**GIFTS:** Cookware, kitchen gadgets, dish towels, dish racks, platters, chef's knives, cookbooks, aged vinegar, and restaurant gift certificates for the cook's night off!

They love to try new restaurants. They watch the Food Network religiously. They are obsessed with immersion blenders. Sound familiar? Then your bride and groom may be perfect candidates for a gourmet kitchen shower. If you have access to a beautiful open kitchen, host the party among colanders and colorful cookware like this set from celebrity chef Rocco DiSpirito. Serve store-bought and homemade delicacies to delight their well-developed palates.

**idea**

Many local cooking schools have professional teaching kitchens that can be rented out for parties. Why not hire a chef to host your gourmet soiree? They can whip up delicious treats right before your eyes, and give your guests tips on how to make magic in their own home kitchens!

# comforts of home

A POTLUCK PARTY OF FAVORITE RECIPES AND HOME-ENHANCING GIFTS

This family-style shower is part recipe exchange, part comfort-food feast, with a little home enhancement thrown into the mix. Ask each guest to bring their favorite dish to serve at the party, and feel free to assign categories, such as "dessert" or "pasta." Include a blank recipe card in each invitation, so that friends and loved ones can help the couple build their repertoire of delicious dishes. This party centers on food, so set up a gorgeous buffet or plan for a family-style dinner at a festive table.

## COZY INSPIRATION

**MOOD:** Rustic, familial, warm, and cozy.

**SETTING:** At home.

**FOOD:** Casseroles, side dishes, salads, pies, and cakes.

**RECIPES:** Tomato Bruschetta, World's Best Mac-n-cheese, Sage-roasted Cornish Game Hens, Garlic-kick Mashed Sweet Potatoes, Gruyère-stuffed Dinner Rolls, Panini Hearts, Mini Peach Upside-down Cakes, Decadent Chocolate Parfaits.

**DRINKS:** Hearty wines with dinner. Rosé Wine Spritzer, Cava Cocktail, Prosecco Pomegranate Punch, Lillet Kiss, White-cranberry Spritzer, Hot Cha-cha-chocolate.

**ACTIVITIES:** Play Cooking Disasters during dinner. Each guest tells a story about a kitchen mishap (one of their own culinary nightmares, or better yet, one of the bride or groom's!). Guests vote on the best story, and the winner gets a wooden spoon, spatula, or other small prize.

**DETAILS:** Use fun dish towels as placemats. Arrange herbs in vases or terra-cotta pots. Place name cards in front of each potluck dish to let guests know who made what ("Aunt June's Famous Peanut-butter Pie").

**GIFTS:** Utensils, cookbooks, platters, comfy throws and pillows, and homemade potholders.

# MENU

Great parties are created by combining great people for a great reason. But give those same fun folks some tasty snacks or a delicious family-style dinner and you've got a surefire recipe for even greater success!

Food is a wonderful means of welcoming and delighting your guests at a wedding shower. Once you've established the theme of your party, think about what style of cuisine best suits the theme (exotic and spicy, dainty and elegant, homey and rustic?). Then combine sensational dishes and creative presentations to add fabulous flavor to your shower.

Remember the first simple stunning rule of successful entertaining: You don't have to make everything yourself! Unless you're very comfortable in the kitchen and you like the idea of cooking all week for your party (as well as decorating and hosting it), choose a few crowd-pleasing dishes you can make easily, and supplement them with high-quality items from your favorite grocery, farmers' market, or restaurant.

When deciding how to serve your group, think about your guest (or guests) of honor, as well as the type of mood you'd like to create. If you're going to host a small, intimate gathering for a group of convivial connoisseurs, a sit-down meal of family-style favorites could be a wonderful idea. If your bride loves Mexican food and margaritas, a simple buffet (and a specialty bar) with her favorites might be just right.

This chapter will give you a head start with some easy, scrumptious recipes, many of which are very quick, and some of which can be prepared in advance to save time on the day of the party. A number of the recipes combine store-bought elements with creative additions to help save time.

The recipes are broken down into four categories: Brunch Bests, Finger Foods, Buffet Favorites, and Sweet Treats. Choose a few you like, and try them out in advance to make sure you're comfortable with the preparation. Don't be afraid to adjust the seasoning to your taste.

## attention host!

The recipes that follow are not just for wedding showers. You can use them anytime you're entertaining friends at home, or for potluck contributions, holiday gifts, or a special treat for yourself on a Tuesday night!

# top five tips for perfect party food

1. **Choose foods that complement your theme and one another.** If you're hosting a Tuscan wine tasting, plan your menu around the flavors of the region—olives, cheeses, hearty breads, grilled vegetables, salami, and pasta. If you're creating a buffet of sweets, go all out with a sumptuous array of cookies, candies, mini tarts, and cupcakes.

2. **Consider your guests.** If you know you'll be hosting vegetarians or guests with dietary restrictions, make an effort to offer at least one dish that will appeal to them. Likewise, if you'll be offering spicy foods, make sure to prepare a tamer dish or two for those who like it "mild, mild, mild!" And always serve foods that are easy to eat in your party's setting; for a cocktail party, serve small portions and avoid messy sauces or super-chewy items.

3. **Don't cook during the party.** Plan your menu around dishes that can be made in advance and served at room temperature or kept warm in an oven until needed. Time flies during a party, and if you spend most of it in the kitchen, you'll miss all the moments you want to share with the guest(s) of honor. A great host spends time with the party guests, not with pots and pans.

tip

Act like a chef. Plan your menu in advance, and have all your ingredients ready for each dish (sliced and diced) before you start cooking. French chefs call this *mise en place*, (everything in place).

4. **Remember, *presentation* starts with *present*.** Think of the foods you offer at your shower as little gifts to your guests, and present them all beautifully. This doesn't require over-the-top designs or expensive serving pieces: Line simple trays with pretty paper, or turn shells upside-down to create bite-size bowls for seafood salad. Garnish cakes with sugar flowers, which are available at cake-decorating stores. Use flower pots as pedestals for your platters to create varying heights on your buffet. Arrange dumplings on inexpensive Chinese spoons and line them up on a rectangular plate.

5. **Place snacks here and there throughout your party space.** Sometimes guests get stuck in one area while visiting with one another, and sometimes the buffet is just too crowded. Set out bowls of nuts or candies all around your home or party location, and make smaller plates of your hors d'oeuvres to accent coffee tables or end tables. Don't forget to include a stack of cocktail napkins and toothpicks and any other items that will help guests enjoy their treats tidily.

Clustering one type of platter in varying sizes makes a beautiful buffet presentation.

# aunt maureen's fluffy egg casserole

Serves 8–10

This is a fantastic party dish, because you do all the work the night before and simply pop it into the oven an hour before your party. It holds up well on a buffet and is tasty even at room temperature.

¼ cup butter, softened

1 large challah bread loaf, sliced (or substitute a fluffy white bread)

½ pound cremini mushrooms, chopped

1 red pepper, chopped

6 scallions, chopped

1 pound shredded cheese
(I like equal parts cheddar, Monterey jack, and american, but Swiss works well, too.)

Salt and pepper

1 dozen eggs

1½ cups evaporated or whole milk
(or substitute low-fat milk)

Preheat oven to 350°F. Butter all the slices of the challah bread. Use remaining butter to grease a 3-quart casserole. Combine mushrooms, red pepper, and scallions in a bowl, and set aside. Layer bread slices to cover bottom of dish.

Spoon half the vegetable mix on top of the bread layer, and sprinkle half the shredded cheese on top of the vegetables. Season with salt and pepper. Repeat with another layer of bread, topping it with vegetables and cheese and seasoning with salt and pepper. Beat the eggs with the milk, and pour the egg mixture over the casserole layers. Cover with plastic wrap and refrigerate overnight.

The next morning, cover with foil and bake for 1 hour and 15 minutes, till fluffy. Let stand for at least 10 minutes before serving.

# quick cranberry-corn muffins

Makes 12–16 muffins

This recipe combines store-bought muffin mix with a few ingredients to make the muffins feel homemade. Their small size makes them perfect for a party.

1 package corn-muffin mix

½ cup canned or fresh sweet corn

¼ cup dried cranberries, plus 2 tablespoons

Prepare muffin batter according to instructions, under-mixing slightly. Add in corn and ¼ cup cranberries, and combine. Batter should still be slightly lumpy (over-beating makes muffins tough).

Pour batter into greased muffin tins. Add a few cranberries on top for garnish. Serve warm or at room temperature.

# nectar of the goddess yogurt salad

Serves 6–8

This is a great do-it-yourself brunch treat that works well for a buffet. The key is to use high-quality honey and Greek yogurt, which is truly the most delicious yogurt on earth!

16 ounces Greek yogurt

1 jar honey

1 cup fresh strawberries, cleaned and chopped

1 cup fresh blueberries

1 cup fresh raspberries

1 cup fresh or canned pineapple

2 cups granola

Juice of one lemon

Place each ingredient in its own bowl. Squeeze lemon juice over all fruits except pineapple. Keep fruits and yogurt refrigerated until serving time. Arrange bowls with serving spoons on a buffet, and invite guests to combine their favorite ingredients.

# panini hearts

*Makes 6 panini*

If you don't have a panini maker (one of my favorite kitchen tools), you can use a grill pan, skillet, or toaster oven to make these decorative, rustic sandwiches. You can fill your panini hearts with any sandwich ingredients you like—cheese, vegetables, ham, turkey, bacon—you name it! They're also fabulous with peanut butter and bananas, or as dessert s'more sandwiches.

2 medium tomatoes, sliced

¼ cup balsamic vinegar

1 teaspoon dried oregano

Salt and pepper

1 loaf of rustic whole wheat or sourdough bread, sliced

2 tablespoons extra-virgin olive oil

1 pound fresh mozzarella, sliced

12 fresh basil leaves

Place the tomato slices in a mixing bowl. Pour the balsamic vinegar over the tomatoes and add the dried oregano. Season with salt and pepper, and turn the tomatoes over a few times to let them soak up the vinegar mixture. Set aside to marinate.

With a heart-shaped cookie cutter, cut out 12 bread hearts. Brush lightly with olive oil. Lay the hearts out on a countertop or tray, and assemble the sandwiches. Start with one sliced bread heart, and top with mozzarella cheese slices, marinated tomato slices, a few basil leaves, and more mozzarella. Top with another sliced bread heart.

Press the sandwiches in a hot panini maker or preheated grill pan over medium heat. If using a grill pan, press down on the sandwiches with a spatula or flat-bottomed baking dish to create that "panini" look.

## spicy roasted cocktail nuts

Makes 11 ounces

These spicy and sweet treats will be a hit at any party. They also make great holiday gifts or favors, packaged in small boxes or tins.

1 can (11 ounces) salted mixed cocktail nuts

2 tablespoons maple syrup

1 tablespoon bourbon

2 tablespoons brown sugar

2 teaspoons cayenne pepper (more if you'd like them very spicy)

2 teaspoons fresh rosemary, finely chopped

Salt

Preheat oven to 400°F.

Pour nuts into a mixing bowl. Combine the maple syrup and bourbon, and pour the bourbon–maple syrup mixture over the nuts; toss to coat. Add the brown sugar, cayenne pepper, and rosemary. If desired, add a pinch of salt to taste. Toss again to incorporate the flavorings.

Spread the nut mixture into a thin layer on a cookie sheet. Roast for 10–15 minutes. Serve warm or at room temperature.

# salty-sweet cheese popcorn

Makes 6 cups

This popcorn is great anytime and is so quick to prepare.

1 package microwave popcorn

2 tablespoons brown sugar

Salt

½ stick butter, melted

¼ cup grated Parmesan cheese

Pop the popcorn. Meanwhile, add the brown sugar and salt (to taste) to the melted butter. Drizzle the salty-sweet butter over the popcorn, top with Parmesan cheese, and serve.

# cucumber canapés

Makes 20 canapés

Typically, canapés are small pieces of bread cut into pretty shapes and topped with any number of ingredients to create a perfect one-bite treat. To save time, buy cocktail rounds or cocktail breads in white, rye, or pumpernickel. These tiny loaves are already cut to the ideal canapé proportions. If you don't have cocktail bread, just use a cookie cutter to cut out your favorite shapes.

1 package white-bread cocktail rounds

2 tablespoons melted butter

1 teaspoon garlic powder

1 medium cucumber, finely diced

1 small sweet pickle, finely diced

Kosher salt

1 tablespoon sour cream

1 tablespoon cream cheese

1 scallion, finely chopped

Preheat oven to 375°F. Brush 20 cocktail rounds with butter on one side, and sprinkle each round with a pinch of garlic powder. Place the rounds on a baking sheet and toast for 3 minutes or until golden.

In a small bowl, combine the diced cucumber and sweet pickle. Season with salt if necessary (the pickle will already add a measure of saltiness). Spoon the cucumber-and-pickle mixture onto a paper towel to drain.

In another bowl, combine the sour cream, cream cheese, and scallions. Spread each cocktail round with the cream-cheese mixture, and top with a small spoonful of the cucumber mix.

# beef canapés with horseradish

Makes about 20 canapés

This crowd-pleaser is like a mini steak sandwich.

¾ pound stew meat, cut into 2-inch cubes

Salt and pepper

1 tablespoon garlic powder

2 tablespoons olive oil plus 1 teaspoon

¼ cup soy sauce

¼ cup balsamic vinegar

1 loaf rye cocktail rounds or squares

1 tablespoon dried tarragon

3 tablespoons horseradish

Preheat oven to 375°F. Season the beef cubes with salt, pepper, and garlic powder. Pour 2 tablespoons olive oil in a skillet and warm over medium heat. When the pan is hot, add the beef cubes and sear them till golden brown on all sides (approximately 3–5 minutes).

Meanwhile, in a small bowl, combine the soy sauce and balsamic vinegar. When the beef is cooked, transfer the meat to a cutting board and cut each cube into thin slices. Add slices to the bowl with the balsamic-soy mixture, and let stand for five minutes.

While the beef is marinating, brush the cocktail rounds with 1 teaspoon olive oil, and season with salt and dried tarragon. Toast for 3 minutes in the oven.

To assemble the canapés, place one slice of the marinated beef atop each toasted cocktail round. Finish with a small dollop of horseradish.

idea

Try these other creative canapé combinations:

- smoked salmon and caviar on pumpernickel
- shrimp salad on white
- toasted ham and gruyère cheese on rye

# tomato bruschetta

Makes about 12 pieces

Bruschetta is Italy's rustic answer to the canapé. Instead of delicate rounds, bruschetta are thicker slices of toasted bread topped with almost anything you like, and served warm or at room temperature. For best results, use small pieces of hearty bread, and feel free to either leave the crusts on or cut them off, as you like. You can toast the bread early in the day and make and refrigerate the topping. Then assemble the bruschetta just before the party starts.

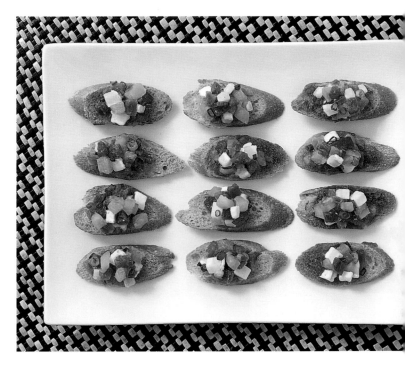

1 long baguette

3 tablespoons extra-virgin olive oil

1 large ripe yellow tomato, diced

1 large ripe red tomato, diced

1 medium-sized ball of fresh mozzarella, diced

1 tablespoon balsamic vinegar

Salt and pepper

2 chives, finely chopped

Preheat oven to 400°F. Slice the baguette fairly thin, on an angle, to create a larger surface for the toppings. Brush the top side of each piece with extra-virgin olive oil, and toast lightly for approximately 3–5 minutes. Let the toasted bread cool before adding the toppings.

In a mixing bowl, combine the yellow and red tomatoes and the mozzarella. Add the remaining extra-virgin olive oil and the balsamic vinegar. Season with salt and pepper and toss. Spoon enough topping over each piece of bread to cover it, but don't overload the bruschetta. Sprinkle chives over the top of each piece, and arrange on a simple platter. Then smile and say, "Ciao, bella!"

**TIME-SAVER:** Use store-bought bruschetta topping. Most good grocers have hearty tomato-based spreads, loaded with herbs and spices, that are made specially for bruschetta.

# lemongrass shrimp skewers

Makes 12 skewers

Transform ordinary shrimp into a wedding shower–worthy dish! The presentation of this dish on lemongrass skewers makes an instant appetizer look stylish and fancy, and the lemongrass adds a light, exotic flavor. Two important tips: First, buy lemongrass stalks that are thick and strong, so they'll work well as skewers. Second, select medium to large shrimp that will retain their shape when skewered.

½ teaspoon salt

½ teaspoon black pepper

½ teaspoon garlic powder

½ ground ginger

½ teaspoon cayenne pepper (if you like it spicy!)

12 medium to large fresh shrimp, peeled and deveined

12 stalks lemongrass

½ tablespoon peanut oil

Juice of half a lemon

In a small bowl, mix the salt, pepper, garlic powder, ground ginger, and cayenne pepper and set aside.

Rinse shrimp in cold water and pat dry. Wash lemongrass and remove any leaves from the stalks. Pat dry, then trim the ends of the lemongrass stalks to form a point. Using a paring knife, puncture each shrimp to make it easier to insert the lemongrass skewers. Insert one lemongrass skewer through each shrimp so that the shrimp is held securely in place. Place the skewers on a baking sheet.

Brush each shrimp with peanut oil on both sides. Sprinkle the spice mix over all the shrimp, then turn the shrimp over and repeat.

In a wide, nonstick skillet over medium-high heat, sear the shrimp on one side until lightly golden. When the shrimp are seared on one side (approximately 1–2 minutes), turn them over in the skillet and sear the other side. Squeeze the lemon juice over the shrimp, and then remove them from the pan. Arrange the skewers on a decorative platter, and serve them warm or at room temperature.

# smoked salmon roll-ups

Makes 18 pieces

These are fancy looking and easy to make, and there's no cooking required!

8 ounces smoked salmon, thinly sliced

4 ounces cream cheese with chives

Juice of 1 lemon

32 capers

18 chives, each at least 5 inches long

Cut salmon slices into pieces roughly 3 inches long by 1 inch wide. Dice up any salmon scraps and add these to a mixing bowl with the cream cheese.

Brush each salmon slice with lemon juice. Then spoon about a teaspoon of the cream-cheese mixture at one end of the salmon slice. Place two capers on top of the cream cheese, and roll the salmon slice until it's wrapped completely around the cream cheese. Secure the bundle with a chive, tying it in a knot.

# tarragon chicken tea sandwiches

Makes 10 sandwiches

The secret to these dainty sandwiches is to buy prepackaged miniature sliced bread, which is available in most good grocery stores and generally comes in white, wheat, rye, and pumpernickel. You can make the sandwiches early in the day and keep them in the refrigerator, covered with a moist paper towel and plastic wrap to prevent drying. Take them out a half hour before the party and display on a tiered stand or silver tray lined with delicate doilies. (See photo on page 32.)

2 boneless, skinless chicken breasts, roasted

10 grapes, quartered

2 stalks celery, sliced

1 teaspoon fresh tarragon

2 tablespoons mayonnaise

1 teaspoon lemon juice

Salt and pepper

1 loaf miniature sandwich bread, white

Shred the chicken and place in a large bowl. Add the grapes, celery, tarragon, mayonnaise, and lemon juice. Season with salt and pepper and stir gently to mix. Top half of the bread slices with the chicken salad, then use remaining slices to form sandwiches. Slice diagonally to create triangular halves.

# nutty goat-cheese morsels

Makes approximately 16 morsels

Work in small batches, keeping the remaining cheese refrigerated: colder cheese makes for easier rolling.

½ cup salted walnuts or hazelnuts

8 ounces goat cheese

Grind the nuts in a food processor until medium-fine, and transfer onto a flat, wide plate. Form the goat cheese into 1-inch round balls, then roll the balls in the ground nuts to cover. Keep the morsels covered and refrigerated until serving time.

# bacon-wrapped dates

Makes 20 dates

Make the bundles ahead, and reheat before the party.

20 dates, pitted

20 almonds, shelled

10 slices bacon

Preheat oven to 400°F.

To pit dates, run a knife down one side lengthwise and split open. Pull out the nutlike pit and discard, then replace pit with an almond and press the date back together.

Cut the bacon slices in half. Wrap each date with half a bacon slice, and secure with a toothpick. Roast in the oven for approximately 15 minutes, turning once to make sure both sides are golden brown. Serve warm.

## world's best mac-n-cheese

Serves 8

A rich, delicious version of the classic comfort-food favorite. Use your favorite pasta shape for a new twist.

Salt and pepper to taste

1 tablespoon olive oil

1 pound elbow macaroni, fusilli, or rigatoni

8 ounces grated cheddar cheese

6 ounces grated Parmesan cheese

4 ounces shredded mozzarella cheese

4 ounces crumbled Gorgonzola cheese

6 ounces ricotta cheese

1 egg

½ cup heavy cream

1 tablespoon garlic powder

4 tablespoons butter

1 tablespoon dried oregano

Preheat oven to 375°F. Fill a heavy stockpot with water and bring to a boil. Add salt to season the water, and olive oil to keep the pasta from sticking. Add pasta and cook for approximately 8 minutes, until al dente. Drain pasta and set aside.

Meanwhile, mix cheddar, Parmesan, mozzarella, and Gorgonzola cheeses in a small bowl, and set aside. Combine the ricotta, egg, heavy cream, and garlic powder in another mixing bowl. Grease a 3-quart casserole dish with 1 tablespoon butter.

In a large skillet, melt 2 tablespoons butter over low heat. Place the cooked, drained pasta in the pan, and add the ricotta mixture, the remaining butter, and the dried oregano. Add three-quarters of the cheese mixture, and stir until cheese begins to melt. Season with salt and pepper to taste. Pour into the casserole dish, and top with the remaining cheeses.

Cover with foil and bake for approximately 30 minutes. Uncover and bake for 5–10 minutes more, until cheese is golden. Let stand for at least 10 minutes before serving.

# sage-roasted cornish game hens with creamy garlic

Makes 6 hens

This dish is at once homey and impressive. Your guests will think you went to a lot of trouble, but in fact, it's very easy to prepare. Toss in the garlic cloves 15–20 minutes before the hens are finished and you'll have a creamy roasted-garlic-clove garnish that guests can mash and spread on their bread or enjoy with the meat.

6 Cornish game hens (1½–2 pounds each)

Salt and pepper

2 tablespoons melted butter, or extra-virgin olive oil

24 fresh sage leaves, stems removed

12 slices bacon

12 garlic cloves, unpeeled

Preheat oven to 350°F. Season the Cornish game hens with salt and pepper on both sides, and place them, breast side up, in a large roasting pan. Truss the legs with kitchen twine, and tuck the wings behind the breasts.

Drizzle the melted butter or olive oil over the birds, and place four sage leaves on each bird, one on each breast and leg.

Next, wrap two slices of bacon around each hen, covering the sage, and stretch the bacon strips to secure them under the bird.

Roast for 45 minutes. Then add the unpeeled garlic cloves to the roasting pan, and cook the hens and the garlic for 15–20 more minutes, until done. Serve each hen with two garlic cloves.

# saffron couscous

Serves 6–8

This savory-sweet, exotic side dish lends any buffet a festive accent.

2 cups chicken stock (or substitute vegetable stock)

1 teaspoon saffron

2 cups couscous

2 carrots, peeled, cooked, and sliced

¼ cup pine nuts

¼ cup currants or raisins

1 tablespoon garlic powder

Salt and pepper to taste

3 scallion greens, finely sliced

Bring the chicken stock to a boil. Add the saffron, then the couscous. Remove from heat, stir, and cover. Let stand for 5 minutes. After 5 minutes, transfer couscous to a mixing bowl and fluff with a fork. Add the carrots, pine nuts, currants, garlic powder, and salt and pepper to taste. Garnish with scallion greens.

# gruyère-stuffed dinner rolls

Makes 8 rolls

If you don't have gruyère, you can use cheddar, goat cheese, or any cheese you like. Also, feel free to add olives, roasted peppers, or crispy bacon. . . . Use your imagination! (The photo to the right shows the rolls with olives and roasted peppers.)

8 dinner rolls (sourdough or whole grain)

4 tablespoons extra-virgin olive oil

¾ cup shredded gruyère cheese

¼ cup grated Parmesan

Salt

2 tablespoons fresh parsley, chopped

Preheat oven to 400°F. Make two cuts halfway through each roll to form an X. Drizzle the inside of each roll with olive oil. Stuff the gruyère inside the roll.

Sprinkle with Parmesan cheese, a pinch of salt, and parsley. Bake for 3–5 minutes, until cheese is melted and light golden brown. Serve warm.

# garlic-kick mashed sweet potatoes

Serves 6–8

This sweet and savory side dish is healthy and comforting. The garlic cloves cook with the sweet potatoes, and if you wait until they're cooked to peel the potatoes, you'll find the skins come off as easy as pie.

3 pounds sweet potatoes

3 garlic cloves, peeled

1 teaspoon nutmeg

2 tablespoons butter

¾ cup evaporated milk

Salt and pepper

Quarter the sweet potatoes. Place them in a heavy stockpot full of cold water. Add the peeled garlic cloves and bring to a boil over high heat. Continue cooking approximately 15–20 minutes, or until tender.

Drain and peel the potatoes, reserving the garlic.

In a mixing bowl, combine the sweet potatoes and garlic. Add the nutmeg, butter, and evaporated milk, and season with salt and pepper. Mix in an electric mixer until mashed.

# sweet treats

## mini peach upside-down cakes

Makes about 12 mini cakes

If you enjoy making cakes and muffins, consider buying some cake-release gel from your local bakers' supply store. It's a premade cake-pan greaser with flour mixed in, and it will help free your cakes from the baking pan. Use it even on nonstick pans. These quick cakes look luxe, and the peaches and brown sugar keep them moist and sticky. Add a sugar rose for garnish!

1 package white or yellow cake mix

¼ cup vegetable oil (or cake-release gel)

½ cup brown sugar

1 cup fresh ripe peaches or canned peaches

Edible sugar flowers for garnish (optional)

Preheat oven to 375°F. Prepare cake mix according to package instructions. Grease a muffin tin with the vegetable oil or the cake-release gel, and sprinkle brown sugar to coat the bottom of each cup. Arrange a few peach slices on top of the brown sugar in each cup, and pour the cake batter over the peaches and brown sugar, filling just over halfway.

Bake cakes for 10–13 minutes, or until the centers are cooked and the sides come away from the muffin cups. Let cool for 5 minutes, then turn out onto a cake stand and garnish with edible sugar flowers.

# green-tea cake

Serves 8–10

This cake is earthy and exotic—perfect for an Asian-inspired party, a spa lunch, or a tea party. You can serve it simply with a drizzle of honey and a sprinkling of powdered sugar, or top it with your favorite vanilla icing and add a scoop of frozen yogurt or green-tea ice cream.

1¾ cups cake flour

1½ teaspoons baking powder

½ teaspoon salt

1 tablespoon green-tea powder (available at Asian markets and gourmet stores)

⅓ cup unsalted butter, plus 1 tablespoon for greasing baking pan

1 cup sugar

3 eggs

1 teaspoon vanilla extract

½ cup crème fraîche (or substitute sour cream or yogurt)

½ cup ground walnuts

2 tablespoons honey for garnish

1 tablespoon powdered sugar for garnish

Preheat oven to 350°F.

In a bowl, combine the flour, baking powder, salt, and green-tea powder, and set aside.

With one tablespoon of the butter, grease a 9-inch square or round cake pan. In an electric mixer, combine the remaining butter and the sugar, mixing until creamy. Mix in the eggs one at a time until incorporated. Add the vanilla. Stir the flour–green tea mixture into the butter mixture, one-third at a time, alternating with the crème fraîche. Fold the walnuts into the batter.

Pour batter into the baking pan and bake for approximately 40 minutes or until a toothpick inserted into the center of the cake comes out clean. Let cool on a wire rack for approximately 10 minutes, then turn cake out onto a serving dish. Let cake finish cooling. To serve, drizzle honey on top of each slice and finish with a dusting of powdered sugar.

## did you know?

**GREEN-TEA POWDER**, known as maacha, is part of the traditional Japanese tea ceremony, and is also used to make green-tea ice cream.

**CRÈME FRAÎCHE** is a thickened cream—imagine combining whipping cream with buttermilk. It's available in most good grocery stores and is wonderful in this recipe or in mashed potatoes or as an accent on hors d'oeuvres and canapés.

# princess parfaits

Makes 24 parfaits

Make these magical petite parfaits the night before and keep refrigerated. Serve in shot glasses or mini plastic cups with spoons.

3 thick slices raisin pound cake

½ cup vanilla soy milk (or substitute evaporated milk)

½ cup graham-cracker crumbs

One 6-pack of vanilla-pudding snack cups

½ cup walnuts, crushed

Cut the pound cake into half-inch cubes and place in a mixing bowl. Pour the soy milk over the cake and toss. Arrange shot glasses or plastic cups in a row on a tray or counter, and build your parfaits: Sprinkle a few graham-cracker crumbs, followed by a dollop of pudding, in the bottom of each cup. Add a small spoonful of the milk-soaked cake and a few crushed walnuts. Repeat the process to create a second layer. Refrigerate for at least half an hour before serving.

## shopping for A CAKE

If you don't have time to bake a cake, take a look around at local pastry shops and groceries. Many fine bakeries have wedding shower designs or can create a theme cake to suit your party. The simplest store-bought cake can be accented with edible flowers from your local fancy food shop or you can find sugar flowers at pastry-supply houses. The cake pictured here was cleverly adorned with valentine message hearts which are served as a garnish with each sweet slice.

# decadent
# chocolate parfaits

Makes 24 mini parfaits

These frozen parfaits will delight chocolate lovers of all
ages.

3 thick slices chocolate pound cake

½ cup chocolate milk

½ cup white-chocolate chips

1 pint chocolate ice cream, slightly softened

1 cup chopped chocolate candy bars (Snickers, Twix, or
    your slightly crunchy favorite)

Cut the pound cake into half-inch cubes and place in a
mixing bowl. Pour the chocolate milk over the cake,
and toss. Arrange small cups or shot glasses in a row on
a tray or counter, and build your parfaits: Sprinkle a
few white-chocolate chips in the bottom of each cup,
followed by a small scoop of the softened ice cream.
Add a sprinkle of the chopped candy bars, then a small
spoonful of the milk-soaked cake. Repeat the process
to create a second layer, and finish with a sprinkle of
the chopped candy bars for garnish.

    Cover tightly and freeze. Remove from freezer a
few minutes before needed to allow ingredients to
soften slightly.

# buying your
# SWEETS

Creating a sweets buffet is a festive option
for any shower theme, whether it's the
centerpiece of your refreshments or an after-
dinner accent. If you like to bake, try some of
the recipes in this chapter. For a no-fuss
alternative, choose a theme (chocolate, for
example, or Italian pastries) and assemble
your buffet with store-bought treats. For
the White Magic shower pictured here, we
found every single cookie, cupcake, and
nibble at a neighborhood grocery store. Use
your décor to enhance your theme.

# melted-chocolate croissants

Makes 10 croissants

These fluffy, decadent treats are perfect for brunch or dessert with a scoop of vanilla ice cream.

10 croissants
5 dark-chocolate bars, broken into squares
1 jar gourmet chocolate sauce

Preheat oven to 350°F. Cut each croissant in half lengthwise, and place chocolate squares over the bottom half of each, leaving a little space at the edges for the chocolate to melt. Warm the croissants in the oven for approximately 5 minutes, until the chocolate is melted. Meanwhile, warm the chocolate sauce on the stove top over low heat. Next, remove the croissants from the oven, and drizzle the melted chocolate sauce over croissants.

# lightning chocolate raspberry cupcakes

Makes about 12 cupcakes

If you don't have time to bake from scratch, here's a great way to transform a store-bought cake mix into something special.

1 package chocolate cake mix
1 jar raspberry preserves
1 can chocolate or vanilla icing
Fresh raspberries for garnish

Line cupcake tins with paper or aluminum-foil cupcake holders, and prepare cupcakes according to package instructions.

Allow baked cupcakes to cool, and cut a funnel-shaped piece of cake out of the top of each, reserving the funnels. Then, fill the funnel hole with the raspberry preserves, replace the funnels atop the cupcakes, and ice with chocolate or vanilla icing. Garnish each cupcake with a fresh raspberry.

# mix it UP

Cheers! Signature cocktails and festive nonalcoholic drinks make every party more fun. When you coordinate them with your party's theme or colors, they also add a vibrant design element. If you're new to the art of mixology, try out a few recipes in advance, or create your own favorites. Here are some tips for serving perfect drinks at your shower:

- Make at least one specialty cocktail to match the theme of your celebration.
- Create a festive nonalcoholic cocktail for your guests who don't drink, and garnish it with pretty candy, a fruit wedge, or umbrella.
- If you expect more than eight guests, consider hiring a bartender to help you mix, serve, and clean up.
- If you're hosting a coed shower, make sure to have the groom's favorite libation on hand, whether it's root beer or bourbon.
- Serve any potent cocktails in small portions, and be sure to have food available throughout the shower.

# sparkling cocktails & punches

SIMPLE STUNNING WEDDING SHOWERS

# prosecco pomegranate punch

Serves 8

Prosecco, a sparkling Italian wine, lends a festive spirit to any get-together. Feel free to substitute champagne. Prepackaged pomegranate juice (much easier than juicing a pomegranate!) is available at grocery stores. Look for the Pom brand pomegranate-tangerine blend.

Two 750-milliliter bottles prosecco

12 ounces Pom pomegranate-tangerine juice

4 ounces brandy

2 ounces Grand Marnier (orange liqueur)

2 tangerines, sliced into rounds for garnish

Raspberries for garnish

Combine all the liquid ingredients in a punch bowl. Stir, and add the tangerine rounds. Keep a bowl of fresh raspberries next to the punch bowl, and garnish cups or glasses with a few berries.

> **hint**
> Prosecco and cava are often less expensive than champagne and make great mixers. They're also wonderful on their own!

# bubbly bride

Makes 4 drinks

Fizzy and a bit sweet, this cocktail is a lovely blue color.

4 ounces vodka

4 ounces white-cranberry juice, plus 1 ounce for coating rims

Pinch of blue decorating sugar for rims

4 tablespoons club soda

4 dashes blue curaçao

In a cocktail shaker, combine the vodka and cranberry juice. Brush the rims of 4 coupe champagne glasses or martini glasses with white-cranberry juice and dip in blue sugar to coat. Pour the vodka and cranberry mixture into glasses and top off with the club soda. Then add a dash of the blue curaçao, and stir gently.

# cava cocktail

Makes 8 cocktails

Cava is a sparkling Spanish wine for which you can substitute champagne or prosecco if you prefer. The results are a fresh twist on the classic bellini.

16 tablespoons peach nectar

One 750-milliliter bottle cava

Fill each champagne coupe or flute with 2 tablespoons peach nectar. Top off with cava, and stir.

## fred & gingertini

Makes 4 'tinis

This fun, crisp cocktail will make guests feel like dancing.

6 ounces gin

2 ounces ginger ale

Juice of one lime

4 lime wedges for garnish

In a mixing glass filled with ice, combine the gin, ginger ale, and lime juice. Strain into martini glasses and garnish with lime wedges.

## saketini

Makes 4 cocktails

Add a bit of exotic, savory flavor to your wedding shower.

4 peeled cucumber slices

2 ounces sake (plus extra for soaking cakes)

6 ounces vodka

Soak the cucumber slices in sake. Pour sake and vodka into a cocktail mixing glass, stir, and then strain into a chilled martini glass or sake cup. Garnish with the sake-soaked cucumber.

## bridal sweet

Makes 4 cocktails

Its pretty red color and sweet taste make this the perfect party drink (pictured here).

6 ounces vodka

2 ounces strawberry juice

1 ounce cranberry juice

Juice of half a lime

In a mixing glass filled with ice, combine all ingredients, and stir. Strain into martini glasses.

# lillet kiss

Makes 4 cocktails

Lillet is a light, refreshing French aperitif made from wine and fruit liqueurs.

12 ounces white Lillet
2 ounces apricot nectar
4 ounces club soda
4 dried apricots for garnish

Combine the white Lillet and the apricot nectar, and divide the mixture evenly into four ice-filled glasses. Add 1 ounce of club soda to each glass, and stir. Garnish each glass with a dried apricot.

# mocha liqueur cups

Makes 12 drinks

Tiny chocolate cups made especially for cordials and liqueurs are perfect for festive occasions. Search the Internet for "chocolate liqueur cups," or see the Resource Guide. Not only are the cups elegant, but there's no messy cleanup, because the guests eat them!

12 dashes brandy

12 chocolate liqueur cups

12 tablespoons coffee liqueur, such as Kahlúa or Tía Maria

Pour a dash of brandy into each chocolate cup. Add a dash of coffee liqueur. Serve on a festive tray.

# rosé wine spritzer

Makes 8 spritzers

Wine spritzers are all the rage again. They're light and refreshing, and the rosé wine adds a slightly fruity quality and a pale blush hue.

One 750-milliliter bottle dry rosé wine

2 tablespoons grenadine

16 ounces club soda

8 lemon twists or fresh strawberries for garnish

Mix the wine and grenadine in a pitcher and keep on ice. When ready to serve, pour into ice-filled glasses and add 2 ounces club soda to each glass. Add a lemon twist or fresh strawberry garnish.

## hot cha-cha-chocolate

Serves 4

Simply the best hot chocolate ever. The key is to use a very high quality hot-chocolate mix. One of my favorites comes from Fauchon, the French confectioner. See the Resource Guide for more information.

4 packages Fauchon hot-chocolate powder (or substitute your favorite brand)

1 pint milk

One 12-ounce can evaporated milk

Pinch cayenne pepper (optional)

20 mini marshmallows for garnish

Pour 1 package hot chocolate powder into each of 4 mugs. In a saucepan, warm the milk and evaporated milk together until the mixture reaches a simmer. Remove from heat, add the cayenne pepper if desired, and stir. Pour milk into mugs, stir, and garnish each mug with 5 mini marshmallows.

tip

Add Kahlúa or Tía Maria to this hot-chocolate recipe for an even more decadent treat!

## white-cranberry spritzer

Serves 6

This crisp drink has all the tartness of regular cranberry juice, without the carpet-staining color!

12 ounces white-cranberry juice

24 ounces lemon-lime soda

6 lime wedges for garnish

Mix the white-cranberry juice with the lemon-lime soda. To serve, pour into wine glasses over ice, and garnish with lime wedges.

# strawberry green-tea cooler

Serves 6

Light and refreshing, with a hint of sweetness, this tea is great anytime.

12 ounces strawberry juice

24 ounces iced green tea

6 fresh strawberries for garnish

Pour ¼ cup strawberry juice into each glass, over ice. Top with the iced green tea, and stir. Garnish with a fresh strawberry.

# orange blossom

Serves 6

Great for a brunch or tea shower, or as a nonalcoholic option anytime. (See photo on page 90.)

6 ounces orange juice

6 ounces tangerine juice

6 ounces guava juice (or substitute cranberry juice)

6 ounces lime juice

6 dashes club soda

Edible rose buds or other edible flowers for
    ice cubes (optional)

Orange juice for ice cubes (optional)

Strawberry Green Tea

Mix the juices together in a pitcher, and add the club soda just before serving. To make floral ice cubes, place small edible petals or blossoms inside ice cube trays filled with orange juice. Freeze cubes and add to beverage just before serving.

Shower games and activities help to break the ice and enhance the party energy. Games typically center around making the bride or couple laugh and blush, and should highlight personal details and fun anecdotes. Activities might involve making a shower scrapbook, writing wishes for the bride and groom, or hiring a magician, fortune-teller, or professional dance teacher to entertain guests.

Choose your games and activities to enhance your shower theme. Customize trivia questions to your travel, home, or gourmet focus. For ladies-only showers, there are many great products, such as Bridal Bingo cards, available on the Internet (see the Resource Guide for more information). If you'll play games that have a winner, make sure to keep little prizes on hand, with extras in case of a tie. For a girly afternoon, create a game-prize grab bag of small tokens like scented soaps, candies, or lip glosses. If your party is coed, offer prizes that appeal to both guys and gals, such as playing cards, CDs, or movie tickets.

# the classics

- **Ribbon Bouquet:** As the bride opens her gifts, guests collect the decorative bows from each package and assemble them into a colorful bouquet for the bride to keep as a happy souvenir of the day, like the one pictured on page 100. To make the bouquet, start with a paper-plate base. Cut a small hole in the center of the plate and thread the ribbon tails through, tying knots on the underside to secure them. You can also staple the bows to the plate, or wire them together with pipe cleaners. In

a charming tradition, the bride often carries this bouquet at the wedding ceremony rehearsal.

- **Wishing Well:** Guests bring small tokens to deposit in a "wishing well" for the bride or couple. Fashion your wishing well out of a glass fishbowl or basket, and decorate it with a festive sign. Gifts for a wishing well are meant to be like stocking stuffers: They are normally brought in addition to the shower gift. Note cards, kitchen gadgets, or travel-sized beauty products are perfect for tossing into the wishing well.

- **Bridal Bingo:** Play this game if you've got a fairly large number of guests, as it will help keep energy high while all those gifts are being opened. Print Bridal Bingo cards on your home computer or buy them on the Internet (see the Resource Guide). Each card should feature a different array of possible shower gifts (pillows, cookware, lingerie, and so on). As the bride opens each gift, guests mark their cards. The first to shout "Bingo!" wins a prize. Continue playing until all the gifts have been opened.

- **Trivia Quiz:** Come up with a list of fun questions to determine how much guests really know about the bride or couple—or how well the bride and groom really know each other. Match your quiz to the theme of your party. If it's a travel shower (see Passport to Love, page 53), ask questions related to the duo's globe-trotting. For an around-the-clock shower (see 24-Hour Shower, page 57) ask time-

**idea**

For a new twist on the wishing well theme, give each guest a pretty four-by-six-inch note card and ask them to write down one wish for the couple. During the shower, the bride draws wishes from the well and reads them aloud, sharing the sweet sentiments with the whole group. Have a store-bought photo album on hand, and slip the cards into the photo holders to create a Book of Wishes for the couple to treasure forever.

These bridal bingo cards, available on the Internet, make gift opening fun for everyone at the party.

Try a Fact-or-Fiction Trivia Test. Describe "facts" about the bride or couple. Guests must decide if the statements are fact or fiction. The winner gets a prize, but everyone gets a laugh trying to figure out what's true and what's a tall tale.

idea

- **Rhyming Toast Challenge:** Great for coed showers. See the Bubbly Brunch shower, page 38.
- **Wedding Singer Karaoke:** See the That's Entertainment shower, page 50.
- **Wedding Wit and Wisdom Book:** See the Double Happiness shower, page 45.
- **Bride and Groom Scavenger Hunt:** See the On the Town shower, page 52.

related questions about the bride and groom. What's their favorite time of day? Their least favorite? Exactly how much time elapsed between their first meeting and their engagement?

# more fresh shower games and activities

- **Make a Shower Scrapbook:** Paste cards, scraps of ribbon, instant photos, and other mementos in an attractive blank journal as a souvenir for the bride and groom.
- **Interactive Favor Bar:** See the Tea & Table shower, page 33, and the Bohemian Bride shower, page 46. Match your favors to your shower theme.
- **Pin the Boutonniere on the Groom:** See the Hours of Flowers shower, page 37.

## playing bridal CHARADES

Divide guests into two teams. The teams alternate turns, with one member pantomiming a word or phrase related to something the bride is fond of. Favorite movie, book, or song titles are great starters, along with phrases like "natural blonde" or the name of her hometown or the place she got engaged. Use a stopwatch to time each team, allowing two minutes for teammates to guess the right answer. The winning team is the quickest team.

Consider hiring a fortune-teller, beauty expert, or other entertainer to add to your activities. A *mehndi* artist can paint pretty designs on ladies' hands as a special treat.

# acknowledgments

I love my job. Not only do I get to design fabulous parties and plan one-of-a-kind weddings—I also have the pleasure of working with the most excellent people who help me make it all possible.

First to my publisher, Leslie Stoker, and to all the wonderful folks at Stewart, Tabori & Chang, including my editor, Jennifer Levesque—a great big thank you for helping me to share the simple stunning message with readers everywhere. To my literary agent, Joy Tutela, and the whole David Black Literary Agency—thanks for everything—literally!

To William Geddes, whose beautiful photographs bring the parties in this book to life—thank you for your talent and your professionalism. Special thanks also to Wick Jackson for his top-notch photographic assistance. To my book designer, Susi Oberhelman, I can never thank you enough for your opinions, your great eye, and all your work to help create the simple stunning look.

Many thanks to my studio staff, whose attention to detail and can-do spirit are invaluable every day, and never more so than in the creation of this book, with its many and varied themes, recipes, and ideas. To Mats Nordman, Brett Underhill, and Lauren Wells, and to each and every one of our interns and freelance pros who've contributed their time and energy—your efforts are greatly appreciated! Special thanks to Chef Alan Tardi for his help with numerous recipes and food styling for the dishes in this book.

Thanks to Lance York and Linda Lieberman at TriServe Party Rentals for their generosity and expertise. Thanks also to everyone at Creative Edge Parties for helping us to create the Cosmopolitan Mix shower.

I am forever indebted to James Brady and his staff at Loft Eleven, Westside Loft, and Penthouse 15 for opening their gorgeous event spaces to our clients and our crew.

Personal thanks and much love to my friends and family. To my sister Sara and her new husband Samir, a big kiss, and a hug for the whole Chokshi family! Thanks to my brother David Bussen for all his good advice about everything, and also to my brothers Josh Bussen and Matthew Bussen. To my best friend Richard Carpiano—thanks for always being there. Don't worry Mr. and Mrs. Carpiano, I'll help Rich when it's time for his wedding!

To Rome Timmons, thank you for your love and support.

Finally, I'm truly grateful to all the brides and grooms I have the pleasure to work with, as well as those I meet and get to know in my travels around the country. Thank you for your love stories, your wedding visions, your excitement, and your kindness.

# resource guide

**PAGE 2:**
Striped pillows, napkin rings, and vase: Crate & Barrel
www.crateandbarrel.com

Gift bags: Paper Presentation
www.paperpresentation.com

Clear glass cylinder bowls:
Jamali Garden Supplies
www.jamaligarden.com

**PAGES 4-5**
China and linens:
TriServe Party Rentals
www.triservepartyrentals.com

**PAGE 7:**
Custom gift wrapping:
Kate's Paperie
www.katespaperie.com

## Getting Started:

**PAGE 8:**
Gift wrap papers:
Paper Presentation
www.paperpresentation.com

**PAGE 11:**
Silk flower petals:
Jamali Garden Supplies
www.jamaligarden.com

## Planning Your Budget:

**PAGE 14:**
Tissue wedding bells:
I Do Foundation
www.idofoundation.org

**PAGE 17:**
Monogrammed candy bars:
Carson Wrapped Chocolates
www.wrappedhersheys.com

**PAGE 18:**
Metal garden pails:
Jamali Garden Supplies
www.jamaligarden.com

Flower workshop invitation:
Luscious Verde
www.lusciousverde.com

## Stunningly Simple:

**PAGE 20:**
Drapes, vase, and punch glass:
Crate & Barrel
www.crateandbarrel.com

Gift wrap papers:
Paper Presentation
www.paperpresentation.com

**PAGE 23:**
Gift bags: Paper Presentation
www.paperpresentation.com

**PAGE 24:**
Bowls, chop sticks, and spoons:
Pearl River
www.pearlriver.com

Vase and candle holder:
Jamali Garden Supplies
www.jamaligarden.com

## Choosing a Theme:

## On the Menu:

## Mix It Up:

## Inspired Fun:

# index

(Page references in *italic* refer to illustrations.)

For more ideas and inspiration, visit us at www.karenbussen.com